"The thie[...]
    steal, an[...]
I have come that they may have life,
    and that they may have it
more abundantly." Jesus (John 10:10)

ALWAYS HERE
FOR YOU

Second Edition

Published by Crossbridge Books
Worcester
www.crossbridgeeducational.com
© Crossbridge Books 2021

First published 2005

ISBN 978 1 913946 66 1

British Library Cataloguing in Publication Data
A catalogue record for this book is available from the
British Library.

ALWAYS HERE FOR YOU

Second Edition

Trevor Dearing

CROSSBRIDGE BOOKS

"He is able to do exceedingly abundantly above all that we ask or think, according to the power that works in us."

(Ephesians 3:20)

CONTENTS

Introduction

From being very young I have had extreme sympathy for those who are suffering from emotional or physical pain. Almost certainly this is because I myself had my first nervous breakdown when I was eleven years of age, and from that time onwards for eight years suffered daily from panic attacks, terrible phobias which I called 'terrors', and sleepless nights, when I tossed in bed, absolutely frightened to death. I was frightened of dying; I was frightened of going blind for some reason, and frightened of going insane, and I suffered also from very deep depression – even at the age of twelve.

1

And so, for eight years my life was a perpetual torment of mental distress and even agony.

I also suffered severe physical pain, because emotional illness can, as we shall see, often intensify, or even cause terrible physical pain. So, I was often absent from school and was very ill as a teenager, and then, at the age of nineteen went to a church for the first time in my life, and Jesus became very real to me. And within a very short space of time, I was completely free of all my illness – both emotional and physical.

I eventually entered first the Methodist ministry and then later the Church of England and was clergyman in four parishes. All this time I maintained pretty good health; I was in good health nearly all the time.

On May 10th, 1969, feeling a very deep compassion for sick and suffering people and

having seen a miracle of healing in a Pentecostal church, I sought the Lord with all my heart with prayer and with fasting to receive the power of the Holy Spirit to enable me to bring healing to those who were suffering terrible sickness.

It was a momentous experience at 40 Deer Park in Harlow, Essex, at about 9 o'clock at night when the room was filled with light and I began to speak in a language I did not understand and to sing with a voice that seemed to be more angelic than my voice, and I saw a huge figure in the distance in white, and I said, "Who are you?" And this voice thundered back: "I am Gabriel, and you are sent to heal the sick."

I eventually began a healing ministry at the parish church of St Paul's in Hainault, Essex, on the outskirts of London, where hundreds of

people came – not only from the local housing estate – from all parts of Britain and different parts of the world, because God was using me miraculously to heal sick people.

Eventually my wife, too, became involved in the ministry, and in 1975, at the suggestion of the Bishop, we began a worldwide ministry of evangelism and healing. This ministry in itself is very demanding, and often I was laying hands on sick people at three o'clock in the morning, sometimes having ministered to hundreds of people, and over the space of a few years these numbers grew to thousands.

I went beyond normal human strength or anything that could be expected of a human being in the workload which I was taking on with desperate people, and eventually it took its toll, so that I collapsed in Dallas, Texas while

leading a healing meeting in 1983. This brought about a complete breakdown of physical and emotional health and once again I suffered mental torment and extreme physical pain for some time. This resulted in my being retired altogether that same year, 1983, from Christian work by the Church of England and the Episcopal Church of America and the Department of Social Security.

However, sickness was not to have the last word, and in 1985, having had many months of terrible ill-health, I was again healed by the Lord; this time when He spoke to me through verse 17 in Psalm 118: 'I shall not die, but live, and declare the works of the Lord.'

For some years I still had to take things slowly, but in 1995 a day of prayer and fasting was organised for me. The Lord graciously granted full healing in response, so I

immediately began the healing work again on an itinerant basis with my wife. Now, as this second edition goes to print, I am eighty-seven years of age and in good health – and still engaged in this healing work.

The counselling for many hours of people coming to our home and our itinerant ministry has brought me into contact with hundreds of suffering people. My ministry is based entirely on sympathy for – and the Greek means 'suffering with' – sick people, and also the insights and the ability of the Holy Spirit which has been given me to help suffering people.

So, I write these pages as a Christian message to you if you are suffering, especially in mind or in body, or know of people to whom you can pass on this little book, and I pray that it will assist them to find God's help and

healing for their emotional and physical condition. And that from gloom and despair and pain and suffering they will find the peace of God and the joy of knowing that they are His children and that they have a purpose in His plan. And that life with Him will be nothing but good and He will lead these healed people on into a relationship with Himself that gives new meaning and purpose to life on earth and in Heaven.

Introduction

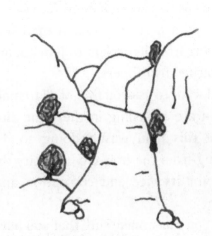

The journey

I am going to base my thoughts to you on the parable of the Good Samaritan, that Jesus told to an expert in the Law who enquired about eternal life, and asked: "Who is my neighbour?"

Jesus, in Luke Chapter 10, verses 25 to 37, told him a story about a man who was journeying from Jerusalem to Jericho, and who was attacked by robbers.

I want to ask you first of all to make sure that you are travelling in the right direction, because this man wasn't doing so. He was travelling from the holy city to a city that was known for its vice and corruption and false religion.

You must make sure that you have done a U-turn, or, as the Bible expresses it, been converted; that you are turning away from the natural way in which human beings go, and have turned to God, with all your heart, mind, soul, and strength; that you are seeking Him alone, or maybe Him alone with the aid of His ministers, to find healing and help.

You must not be looking to New Age teaching, occultism in any of its forms, mediums, spiritualists, or even other religions of the world for your help. If the teaching of this little book is to reach the depths of your being and set you free from emotional and/or physical pain, then you must make sure that your life is turned towards God; and so are journeying from sin and darkness and unbelief towards a heavenly Jerusalem which awaits all those beyond this life who truly know the Lord.

So, this little book is for those who are seeking God – the God who has revealed Himself as our Father in our Lord Jesus Christ. And as you look to Him, and on your journey of life turn towards Him, and keep your mind and your whole being, as far as is possible, fixed on Him, then you will find incredible, indescribable, peace and joy, and health and

strength. No matter how deep your suffering is now – you will find that

> 'believing, you rejoice with joy inexpressible',

says the Bible (1 Peter 1:8) as you seek God on your journey from Jericho to Jerusalem.

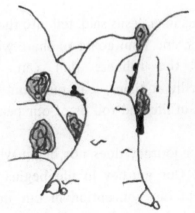

The robbers

On our journey of life – for life *is* like a journey, and each day another mile on the way towards our heavenly Jerusalem – we can indeed fall into the hands of robbers who want to rob us of our health, who want to rob us of our peace,

who want to rob us of our relationship with God.

This man, Jesus said, fell into the hands of robbers; and I am going to share with you some of the robbers that can, almost unexpectedly at times, leap out from behind the rocks of life and rob us of our peace and our joy.

Our journey does not begin when we are born. Our journey in life begins at the moment of our conception in our mother's womb. This is one reason Christians are so opposed to abortion – because we regard it as legalised murder; and indeed, often the act of having an abortion can lead a person away from God and into intense despair and depression, because the instincts of motherhood have been aroused within the pregnant woman. So, if you have ever had an

abortion, then turn to God and say you are sorry that you did so and be sure that He will forgive you and set you on the path of life again towards Him.

However, from the moment of conception, robbers immediately begin their work of destruction and despair. We know that the environment of the womb is vulnerable to damaging influences. This could be in the form of poor or unhealthy nutrition, or even poison, for example from alcohol or substance abuse. Scientists believe that our sense of hearing develops at a very early stage, so that even what is heard from inside the womb could create stress and distress. There is also increasing evidence emerging that the unborn baby can experience physical pain.

So, we need to seek God about even the very first moment of our life, and ask Him to

heal us of anything in that early stage that would incline us towards anxiety or depression, or even physical illness.

Whether we have had an easy passage into this world or a difficult one, these early influences can still affect us even in later life in our emotional wellbeing, and we need to ask the Lord to take us back to the time of our birth (or earlier) and to heal us of anything that would have traumatised us even as we were being born so that we would be inclined to suffer later in life from emotional illness and pain.

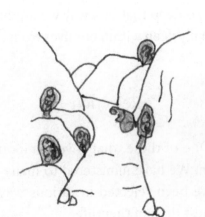

The wounds

Once we have been born into this world, certain attitudes towards us can cause us broken heartedness and bruising; and by 'heart' I mean the depth of our innermost being, which can be severely hurt, or even broken.

And we can be bruised, and we can even have wounds so deep that in a way we are bleeding emotionally deep within our lives from an early age.

Rejection

One of these, that is very important, is rejection. We have ministered to many people who have been rejected in various ways from the earliest days of their life.

We have met young adults, and even older ones, who have told us that their parents deliberately and definitely told them that they were never wanted; that they were a mistake and that the parents wish they had never been born.

Rejection by parents is a fairly common cause of emotional pain – again, even in later

life. Rejection, however, is possible not only by our parents, but by our siblings – those other children in our family who treat us badly; or other relatives who have favourites amongst the family or a particular favourite and make us feel inferior.

This rejection can also be at school; bullying, for instance, is a very sad but common occurrence in schools today. There can be rejection when others are playing games at school, maybe in the playground, and we are left out. At school we can also face rejection even by a teacher who does not like us and makes us feel that way and we are aware that this teacher has very little time for us. The danger of rejection on social media platforms is an emerging issue of our time.

Rejection goes on into teenage life, where once again we find that maybe our

friends have girlfriends or boyfriends, sometimes in serious relationships. Nobody ever seems to want us. Rejection can take place all through life – at university, or at work, where we are made to feel 'no good' as students or at the job that we are doing.

One of the worst forms of rejection is to be rejected by someone we deeply love; maybe even someone we have married, and they walk out on us. Thankfully, such things have never remotely happened to me, but I have met many people who have been terribly, deeply, dreadfully hurt by rejection from the husband or wife whom they deeply love who in the end walks out on them in favour of someone else.

It is sad to say that even church can be a place where we experience rejection. I was once at a meeting of the World Conference of the Holy Spirit in Switzerland, where the

speaker asked any in the congregation of several thousand people to stand, who had been rejected by their pastor or minister or fellow-Christians. And I was amazed to find that two-thirds of the congregation stood to their feet.

When we are in pain emotionally, and seek help, we can be rejected by those who are specifically God's servants, but who do not seem to have time to deal with our deep hurts and emotional pain.

And so, rejection is a robber. Rejections hits us as it were with stones, staves, and clubs deep down inside, and can cause us to feel physical pain nearly all the days of our life.

Insecurity

Another robber that can rob us of our peace from a very early age is to feel insecure, especially as a child. This can be caused almost accidentally by our place in the family, where, for instance, we are born and quickly afterwards, say fourteen months, another child is born to our parents. So, we feel that we have to fight for our place in their affection and feel insecure in their love in comparison to the other child who has been born, or other members of the family.

But the most common cause of insecurity as a child that we have encountered in counselling people has been for a child – maybe you – to be present when mother and father are engaging in the most terrible row: shouting, hysterical outbursts, perhaps the use

of foul language and in some cases even coming to blows. Parents can do this without being aware of the effect they are having on a child – maybe you – as they thrash out their differences of opinion or give vent to their anger with each other.

For a child, especially a young one, although it can affect older ones, to stand in a room and not only once but frequently be present when such anger and violence is being expressed between the mother and father, both of whom they love, can cause terrible hurt and even terror to enter the child's mind.

It is indeed sad that parents can have these dreadful rows without realising that their child, even their young adult child, is not interested in who is right or wrong between their mother and father – all they know is that two people they love equally and as individuals

seem to have made their world fall apart and caused terror and fear to enter their minds.

Being insecure in parental love; being insecure because of parental arguments, disagreements, and even fighting is a common cause of deep-seated feelings of insecurity in a person's life, even in elderly years. The robbers, once again, have leapt upon you, or someone you know, as a child and beaten them inside to make them feel even in later life fear and panic and depression, and intense emotional pain.

Words

Few people really appreciate the power of words, either spoken or written. Words are like books that penetrate the deep inner recesses of a human being's life – at any stage of life – and may explode within the depths of the soul and mind, so that they cause a shattering of security and peace.

Indeed, when we are thinking of robbers, words can be worse than anything else we can experience to cause us pain. Often these words that have been spoken or written to us are remembered by us. Perhaps they have caused intolerable hurt, and they are remembered by us all the days of our life. With contemporary social media, hurtful words are often both public and permanent.

The closer emotionally the person is to us, who speaks bad words deliberately, the more intense the pain will be throughout our lives. And so, although we often remember the words that have been spoken to hurt us very deeply, the human mind has, like the body, defence mechanisms and the mind's defence strategy is to try to forget the words; to try to put them deep down within one's being, so that they do not cause conscious hurt any more. But what we have to appreciate is that although the words themselves may be forgotten, the emotion attached to them can still live on; in fact, almost always does live on deep down, beyond the depths of our memory banks.

And so, we can feel emotional pain without fully realising what is causing it – when it is the robbers: words that have battered us

throughout our lives. And it is these which often are causing someone like you, dear reader, to feel emotional pain.

Deeds

Of course, the robbers in Jesus' parable did perform brutal deeds, literally beating this traveller with clubs or hurling huge boulders at him. Deeds that we have experienced which have been hurtful are again a cause of emotional pain and can be felt throughout our life. What we are thinking about here is how we have been treated, say, by our parents or one parent.

We have counselled people who have been sexually abused – say, young girls, by their father. This sexual abuse is so traumatic that it shatters the innermost peace and wellbeing of any child. It brings with it a sense of shame, and even a sense of guilt. Sometimes we have known a wife cover up these activities by her husband towards a little child, and this

in itself is a dreadful offence against the wellbeing of someone they together have brought into the world.

Deeds may not only involve sexual abuse; they can be physical attacks, doing lasting damage. We have known children who have been beaten, not only with hands, but sometimes with canes or straps – this, again, by someone whom they love; and the pain is not only physical, but also emotional.

We have already seen that words can cause hurt; but how we are treated by our parents; how we are treated by our friends; how we are treated even when we are married, by a son or a daughter; how we treat them; how we treat the person whom our son or daughter has chosen to marry – any of these can cause intense pain.

You may have experienced very poor attitudes and wrongful deeds being performed against you by an in-law or in-laws whom you did not choose to relate to, but found yourself accidentally having to, through marriage. So, deeds can be very cruel; abuse, beating, hurt and pain by acts people have performed against us that have caused us intense shock.

This can have been the deed of a schoolteacher, a relative, a neighbour, a person in authority, or someone we thought was our friend; or it can be the deed of someone we have trusted and respected, who suddenly hurts us intolerably, and again can cause us physical pain and also emotional pain throughout the whole of our life.

Failure

We can also be hurt by failure. Many of us – in fact perhaps all of us – have some goal in mind that we wish to achieve. This can be in the realm of a happy marriage; it can be in the realm of success at school or university; it can be in the realm of our job or our business; and we set these ideals for ourselves even in our Christian life: that we shall be good people and live up to the standards set for us by our Lord Jesus Christ. And then, for one reason or another, we fail to achieve our goals.

This feeling of failure brings with it a dislike – even hatred – of ourselves. We fail to accept ourselves as we are and for what we are. We feel we just make a mess of things, and often the situation is exacerbated by the fact that we are made to feel a failure by parents or

teachers or professors or ministers or those whom we love.

I have often counselled people who experienced this. In fact, I would say that the most frequent cause of depression is lack of self-love. This robs us of our peace. We must remember that our Lord Jesus Christ did not say that we should love our neighbours and not ourselves; He in fact said that we should love our neighbours *as* ourselves. There is a proper self-acceptance of ourselves as we are, with the good things and the limitations that are ours through no fault of our own. Then we must realise that God made us – and God does not make junk! 'I am fearfully and wonderfully made.' (Psalm 139:14) We must love ourselves in a proper manner; accept ourselves, and this can be helped by a loving partner or friend.

We all need praise from time to time, but so many people we have counselled have not had praise, but only condemnation. We also have met women who have a goal, a picture of what they should be like physically, perhaps even men as well may have similar aspirations, and then they find that they have put on a lot of weight. Sometimes this has been caused by comfort eating in a state of depression. This changing of shape; this extra weight that the person is carrying, meaning that they cannot wear the clothes that they would like to wear, or lose their fitness to participate in physically demanding activities, can bring with it a feeling of failure, when we do not like what we see in the mirror.

And so, the sense of self-rejection; the sense of self-condemnation multiplies and grows – it is a robber, that robs us of our peace.

Bereavement

Finally, amongst our robbers is something no one can help, but something that can cause intense sadness – and that is bereavement; the loss through death of a near relative; a child, husband or wife, mother, or father. And the grieving process is a healthy one, but so often it not only brings a sense of irreparable loss, but with it a sense of guilt as to how we have failed in some way the person who has died and is now beyond reparation.

The loss of a loved one can be a terrible blow. For a Christian, as St Paul says, death has lost its sting,

'Death is swallowed up in victory.' (1 Corinthians 15:54).

Death is but the doorway, as it were, into another room; but more than that – into

another dimension of life, full of wonder and rapture and joy. So, if we can accept the Christian message, the loss of a loved one will have lost its sting. But although the Christian message speaks of tremendous hope and expectation for the one who has died, the circumstances of a death can be tragic – if, for instance, a small family is left behind to be cared for by a single parent or perhaps the wage-earner has gone. Death has lost its sting but can still be a robber through the circumstances of the death to rob us of our peace, and we must not try to run away from this, but face it square on with the Christian hope. Remember your feet stand on the rock of solid ground,

> 'The Lord is my rock and my fortress and my deliverer; My God, my strength, in whom I will trust.' (Psalm 18:2)

Storms

To look at another cause of terrible emotional pain, I want to leave behind the parable of the Good Samaritan for a while and turn to another passage in the Bible: St Mark Chapter 4, and read the incident of Jesus being in the boat when the storm arose on the Sea of Galilee. In this short incident we see that there are storms in the natural course of nature on earth. Storms arose on the Sea of Galilee, and still do, without any warning; they just suddenly burst upon that sea in the Holy Land with powerful winds and torrential rain. And so, the disciples had set out on the Sea of Galilee with no sign of any bad weather in sight. Suddenly it comes, and they are terrified, because the boat is filling with water and they

are sinking, and Jesus is asleep on a cushion in the stern. In their terror they wake Him up:

"Teacher! Don't you care that we are perishing?" they shout.

"Why are you so fearful? How is it that you have no faith?" says the Lord. Then He speaks peace to the storm and the waters become calm (Mark 4:35-41). And then He addresses what I believe to Him was more important and more a cause of Divine concern, which was the storm that was going on in the disciples' lives – the fear, the terror, because to be in the middle of a terrible storm on a sea, when there is nothing to hang on to, there is nothing you can cling to; you are simply going down, insecure, and afraid.

It has been my experience that storms can break forth upon people's lives: individuals, families, and even whole

communities. Not just physical storms, although hurricanes and the like do occur, but storms that suddenly burst upon our life such as when we are suddenly bereaved - perhaps when someone has a heart attack through business pressures, without warning. We are threatened; without warning our security is overwhelmed through circumstances that we have not foreseen. Such events as these I call the storms of life – and every one of us will almost certainly experience such a storm, or more than one, in our lives. And we are terror-stricken; we are in terrible emotional pain and panic, and it can even seem to a Christian that Jesus is not concerned; that our Jesus is asleep.

But we need to meditate a lot on this passage and realise that He is not acting, not because He does not care, but because everything is under His control; and we must

listen to Him; trust Him; believe that all will be well; that the events will turn out even for our good; that peace will come as He addresses the storm that has arisen within our lives.

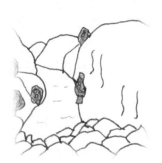

Impediments
To our healing
or
Infections of the wounds from which we are suffering in our soul.

We have seen that hurt, wounding, bruising can be a real part of our mental life that can affect us through the whole of our life. This mental suffering can take the form of phobias,

panic attacks, depression, stress, or even a lapse into schizophrenia, where a person will live in an imaginary world to avoid the pain that has been caused in their minds by the real world.

But if we are to find the healing that God will give us, we must deal with some very definite infections that can invade our wounds and make our suffering and situation very much worse, and make healing from God very, very difficult, if not impossible.

The first of these is that we can nurse bitterness and unforgiveness deep within our souls. And these can, in my experience, be like a cancer that will spread in our being, that will be a kind of malignancy causing all our wounds to be oozing with poison. So, we must get rid of all bitterness and unforgiveness and we must release from any debt to us and from any

41

bondage, all those who have hurt us, whether they are still alive or even passed from this life.

Jesus emphasised the need to forgive very strongly in His teaching in the Gospels. For instance, He told the parable of the unforgiving servant, (Matthew 18:21-35) who, when he had been forgiven so much by his master, as we have been forgiven by God for our sins, refused to forgive someone who had, by comparison, hurt him in a relatively trivial way. Jesus said this man was cast into prison till he could pay all his debts.

This prison we should see as the prison house of depression, or fear, from which we cannot escape. He also, in the Lord's Prayer, taught us to say to our Father, 'And forgive us our debts, as we forgive our debtors,' (Matthew 6:12) and added that if we do not forgive those

who have wronged us, neither will our Heavenly Father forgive us our trespasses.

This condition of bitterness and unforgiveness, deep within the soul, must be dealt with ruthlessly. It must be brought to the surface, and we must really know, from the depths of our being, that we have forgiven those who have hurt us. It is sometimes difficult to do this because we can feel our bitterness and unforgiveness to be fully justified, and indeed it may well be so; but nevertheless, according to the teaching of Jesus there can be no excuse whatsoever for holding on to these terribly negative emotions, that can prevent our healing.

So, search your heart, and even write down on paper as you examine your past life, those who have hurt you; those who have wounded you; those against whom you may

feel bitter and find difficult to forgive. And as you bring each one before the Lord – it may take a little time – when you have truly forgiven that person you can strike a line to obliterate their name from the piece of paper that you have in front of you. Do not let bitterness and unforgiveness ruin your life. They rarely help the person but hurt only you – they will be within you a terrible hindrance to your receiving the forgiveness of God.

Another deep infection in our wounds is unconfessed sin and guilt. Yes, we may try to excuse ourselves, but we do not quite do it. We may feel that yes, we know people who are far worse that we are and have done or said worse things than we have; and so, we seek false ways of trying to get rid of our sin and our guilt. The Bible says, 'If we confess our sins, He is faithful

and just to forgive us our sins and to cleanse us from unrighteousness.' (1 John 1:9)

In counselling, I have found that it has been fairly easy for people to accept the fact that God has forgiven them. It has not been quite so easy, but reasonable, to accept the fact that the person who needed to forgive them has done so - but the thing is a real problem when we cannot forgive ourselves. This is the most common cause of guilt – that we really think that we are better people than to do this or to say this or not to do it. It is an inverted from of pride when we cannot forgive ourselves. We are saying, 'I am too good a person to behave like that.'

It is far better to accept ourselves as sinners that we really are, every one of us; that we really are or were bad enough to do these things or to say them. We need to be like the tax collector in Jesus' parable of the Pharisee

45

and the tax collector. The Pharisee went into the Synagogue and thought he had made it; there was nothing wrong with him; he could look God in the face without embarrassment. He thanked God that he was not a sinner like the tax collector.

But the tax collector was honest, as we should be. He was truly sorry, and said: 'God, be merciful to me a sinner!' Jesus said it was this man who realised that he was a sinner; who realised that he was bad enough to perpetrate evil deeds, to harbour evil thoughts, and to swindle people; that he was, deep in his heart, a sinful man, who cast himself upon the mercy of God.

"I tell you this man," **said Jesus**, "went down to his house justified rather than the other." (Luke 18:10-14) **So let us deal ruthlessly with bitterness and unforgiveness and let us**

equally deal ruthlessly and bring before God
our sin and our guilt.

Another kind of infection in the wounds
of our lives that prevents our healing is self-
pity. To indulge in self-pity or to have what I
call a 'pity party' is the most disintegrating of
the emotions to our personality and our being.
We shall never be well if we engage in it, and it
is a barrier to God's healing, always to be
feeling sorry for ourselves; always seeking
other people's sympathy or attention.

It is important, if we are to experience
God's healing, that we set our will in the
direction of help. It is important that we have
courage and bravery and ask God for strength.
It is important that we trust in the power of the
Lord to heal us, and that our will is set in the
direction of being whole and healthy, and not
to need over-attention from other people

(although seeking other people's help does of course have its place).

Let us remember that it is a rare state for us to be in when there are not thousands of people in the world who would not willingly change places with us in our condition. Let us rather seek to help others; to sympathise with others; to live an outward-looking life of love and help, and not indulge ourselves in sentimental self-pity.

And so, if we can bring before God and get rid of our bitterness and unforgiveness, our sin and our guilt; and if we take courage, and do not engage in self-pity, we shall be well on the way towards mental and physical health, and even more importantly, spiritual health.

The healing
by the good Samaritan

I have read the parable of the good Samaritan many times and seen that this kind, helpful person is really Jesus speaking about Himself. He is the Good Samaritan.

Here is this man, lying on the ground in an utterly helpless condition. He is bleeding and dying on the Jericho road. He cannot do one thing to help himself. He cannot get to his feet; he cannot even cry out for help. The utterly helpless state of this man is something for us to contemplate and often we too feel that we cannot do any more to help ourselves.

We, on the journey of life, are lying helpless; bleeding and dying on the Jericho road; full of pain, and our wounds bleeding as we lie there, unable even to cry out for help. But there is something wonderful in the story of the good Samaritan. Typically, we think of the priest, who walks by on the other side, as representing the established Church, or any church that does not want to be involved with emotionally suffering people, and the Levite as representing a lay person who likewise does

not want to know, and only wants to keep company with those who are well and has no care for those who are in deep distress.

In the Greek, we read that Jesus said the Samaritan "was filled with pity and *approaching* bound up the wounds." (Luke 10:33-34) The good Samaritan came to where the man was, bleeding and dying on the Jericho road. So often we hear evangelists telling us we must come to Jesus, and there is nothing unbiblical or wrong with that call to turn to Christ, but what I see in the good Samaritan is the infinite compassion of God – in that when we are suffering He does not wait for us to come to Him; He comes to us, just where we are on our journey of life; in our suffering and in our pain and helplessness.

I said in the introduction to this book that I was ill myself, emotionally and physically,

and at the age of nineteen I was healed by Jesus. As I look back upon that time, when I sat in a church for the first time in my life, so utterly in emotional and physical pain, I realise that nobody asked me to come to Jesus; no preacher told me to come to Jesus. Jesus came to me where I was, in my suffering; in my sickness; in my depression and in my need.

In the parable, the good Samaritan was crossing every national, racial, and even religious barrier to meet this man's need as he lay helpless on the road. And I want to assure you that as you are in pain, and suffering emotionally and physically, Jesus is with you. Hence the title of this book: **'Always here for you'** – because He is.

Sometimes we are too wounded and too sick and too ill to appreciate Him; and we certainly will not if we engage in self-pity; but

you can be assured that as you are in pain; as you are suffering; and as you feel helpless, the Lord Jesus Christ is with you. He has come to where you are – just where you are on your journey in life, and although you may not feel it, His loving arms are round about you; and although you cannot see them, His compassionate eyes are gazing upon you. Be assured that just where you are on the journey of life, in your suffering and your pain, there has never been and never will be a time when Jesus, the Good Samaritan, could be nearer to you than He is now. He is with you.

Meditate on that truth. Grasp it. Absorb it. To experience it is to realise it in your spiritual imagination, and feel the reality of the love of Jesus, the Good Samaritan for you in your condition; this is itself a powerful source of healing and therapeutic blessing.

The Healing Itself

Jesus is more than with you in spirit, although that is very wonderful. He does more than sympathise with you or gaze upon you; He actually begins, and completes, a healing process.

In this parable, the Greek in which it was originally written reads that the good Samaritan 'bound up the wounds, pouring on oil and wine' (Luke 10:34). He poured the oil and wine into the wounds – into the very depths of where the infection and the pain actually were.

We should realise that the grace and love of God, as we just rest and relax and wait

upon Him, is being poured into the innermost parts of our being. Oil is a soothing balm; in New Testament days the most soothing of all. The wine was a primitive but effective antiseptic to deal with infections.

I just want to share with you that, for the oil and the wine that Jesus pours in to be really effective, firstly the wounds in your innermost being must be exposed. They must be faced; they must be brought to the surface. You may have to spend time alone with a pen and paper in front of you and ask God to reveal the depths of your heart. Read, for instance Psalm 139:13-15, and see how God knows your innermost being and has done since even before you were born:

> 'For You formed my inward parts; You covered me in my mother's womb. I will praise You, for I am fearfully and wonderfully made; marvellous are Your

works. And that my soul knows very well. My frame was not hidden from You when I was made in secret.'

.

As you lay bare your wounds, maybe with tears, and I have known people in terror actually scream, you are exposing them to God. Maybe a counsellor, a good listener, will help you just pour out your heart with its hurts and its wounds as I have already taught. Pour them out.

I have a saying: 'There is nothing hidden that can be healed.' That is why the Bible says we must confess – that is, bring to the surface our sins, before they can be forgiven. If we buried them deep within our souls and tried to excuse ourselves, they would never be healed.

The whole of the Bible's teaching, as we have seen in the parable of the Pharisee and the tax collector, as he exposed his very heart to

God, shows us that it is as we expose our innermost being; as we search our hearts; as we bring things to the light and even write down on paper the things that have caused our wounds; that have hurt us; that have bruised us; that have caused us to be so helpless – it is as we expose them to God, and it may be sometimes with the help of a counsellor, that the oil can be applied. Oil and wine in the Bible are symbols of the Holy Spirit.

The Holy Spirit is a Person of the Trinity who indwells us, so it is very important that you do not try to hide anything from God or yourself, but really open yourself up to God; and the practical thing is to write down on a piece of paper – maybe taking several weeks over it – those things that have hurt you; the people that have hurt you, forgiving them; doing all the things I have taught you in this

book, and letting God the Holy Spirit minister to you. Let a Christian counsellor pray over you.

Another way in which we can let Jesus pour in the oil and wine is deliberately and purposefully to re-live the experiences that have caused our pain and our hurt once we have brought them to the surface of our minds, either in prayer or with the help of a counsellor. We re-live them, go through them, feel the pain of them, feel the hurt of them, and express our emotions without inhibition, but we now do it a different way.

The fact is, that God purposed your birth; you are not in this world by accident, as Paul teaches in his letter to the Ephesians (Chapter 1 verse 4). God planned your birth long before He set the sun ablaze; He was with you, as we have seen in Psalm 139, when you were conceived and being formed in your

mother's womb. Therefore, although you may not have realised it, He has been with you all your life; you may not have been conscious of His presence and tried to face things in your own strength.

Now, in this second way, that should go alongside the first way I've described (bringing your wounds to the surface and praying over them), close your eyes and relax; re-live the experience, but see Jesus in it; see Him coming into your experience, seeing in your spiritual imagination what He is doing; hearing Him speaking words of peace; hearing Him speaking to your troubled heart; seeing how He turns the situation around; seeing how He is right there, at the very time when you were first in pain; and He has been with you all the time. But now, in this quiet time alone with Jesus you re-live the experience and just see what He will do; see

what He will say, because I believe in, and have experienced, and seen in others, the life-transforming power of the presence of Jesus.

Finally, I have for many years taught that the healing of our wounds can take place through deep and quiet meditation on healing promises contained in the Bible. Bible reading is a good thing to do – we should all know our Bible as best we can, just through reading it. Bible study – comparing text with text, either by oneself or in a Bible study group, is even better. But ultimately the best way to use the Bible is to meditate upon passages or upon certain scriptures.

In my book 'The Living Word II', I teach how to use meditation as part of a devotional, based wholly on Biblical Scripture. In my book 'Total Healing' there is also a chapter on how to meditate on the Bible, and I have written many helpful power texts, and taught how these scriptures contain the power to bring about what they promise when they have been absorbed into the very depths of your being over days and days of meditation upon them. And I am now going to repeat most of that chapter from 'Total Healing', which is a book on the healing of the whole person.

Christian Meditation

In the same way that asking God to expose and heal hidden pain in the depths of the soul is a therapeutic spiritual exercise, so too, Christian meditation on scriptures that promise healing is also a practice in which we should all participate. It will bring in-depth peace to our hearts in these days when the speed of life is so fast and pressure intense and stress a common experience. Even more important than this is the fact that this type of prayer will bring in-depth healing by God into the hidden recesses of the soul.

When we engage in this pursuit of peace there are two important promises about the Word of God with which we must begin. The first promise is that:

'The word of God is living and powerful, and sharper than any two-edged sword, piercing even to the division of soul and spirit, and of joints and marrow.' (Hebrews 4:12)

The double-edged sword was the sharpest weapon known in Biblical days. We can today liken it to the sharpness of a surgeon's scalpel. What this scripture is stating, therefore, is that the Word of God can reach the very depths of our being, the division between soul and spirit. It can therefore penetrate the very depths of our soul, reaching down to pre-birth experiences. The second promise is:

'So shall My word be that goes forth from My mouth; it shall not return to Me void, but it shall accomplish what I please, and it shall prosper in the thing for which I sent it.' (Isaiah 55:11)

Here indeed is a precious promise! We are going to meditate on God's Word, and it will accomplish His healing will in our souls. We can draw a parallel here between good medication a doctor may prescribe, and what happens in our souls when we absorb the Word of God. The tablet we take is prescribed to accomplish a certain result in, say, our body. It also has chemical or herbal substances that have power within them to accomplish this end. In a similar way the Word of God has a purpose: to bring us healing deep within our souls, and it is also a **living** and **active** Word, containing within it the power to accomplish this very desirable result.

To absorb God's Word, we must set aside at least fifteen minutes every day, in a private place where we will not be disturbed, having shut ourselves in, to be alone with God.

We remember Jesus' words that God sees in secret and will surely be with us (Matthew 6:6).

We must sit or lie down, relax our bodies, but concentrate our minds on God, remembering that He is very near. We take a text of Scripture, learn it by heart, and repeat it aloud several times. Then we go over it repeatedly, emphasising and thinking about the meaning of each different word or phrase, applying the text to ourselves. For example, we may take Philippians 4 verse 13:

> "I can do all things through Christ who strengthens me."

We first learn this scriptural promise by heart, and then reflect on it again and again, confessing that we – in all our need and weakness, trepidation, and fear – can do everything through Him – Christ – who gives us strength. Then emphasise the word

'everything' – nothing, not even the daunting task we face today, is excluded. Eventually we begin to absorb the fact that this is **through Christ** – spend time thinking about who He is and what the Gospels show He can do – and that nothing is impossible for Him to accomplish. Then we reflect on the fact that, for this issue or task that is so unnerving or frightening, He 'will give me strength – I am not going to undertake it in my own weakness, but in His strength.'

We must meditate on this text for several days in order to absorb its truth and its unfailing promise. We will recall all it means when we feel inadequate, weak, or fearful, or face a task that we feel unable to accomplish. This will mean for an agoraphobic, for instance, going to the shops as on a holiday. In this

context we would do well to remind ourselves also of:

> 'Him who is able to do exceedingly abundantly above all that we ask or think, according to the power that works in us.' (Ephesians 3:20)

There are many other promises God has made that we can learn and on which we can meditate. To take another one, God has promised:

> 'You will keep 'me' in perfect peace, whose mind is stayed on You, because 'I' trust in You.' (Isaiah 26:3)

Notice I have personalised this text to make it applicable to myself. Again, we learn it by heart and repeat it aloud several times. Then word-by-word:

You – we meditate on who God is in His infinite power and love.

will – the absolute certainty of the promise.

keep – the unfailing permanency of the promise.

me – despite my fearful, troubled state of mind.

in perfect peace – what is **perfect** peace? – It is without lack or hindrance – then feel the peace flowing into you and over you.

whose mind is stayed on you – **fixed upon God with no distractions.**

because 'I' trust in You – **because I trust in God I can be assured of His perfect peace.**

Or, slightly differently, Jesus said:

> "Come to Me, all you who labour and are heavy laden, and I will give you rest. Take My yoke upon you and learn from Me, for I am gentle and lowly in heart, and you will find rest for your souls." (Matthew 11:28-29)

Here Jesus is picturing a yoke of oxen dragging a very heavy load up a hill. Do I feel burdened like that? Am I labouring under a load of care

or depression I feel I cannot bear? I grasp the invitation to come to Jesus and think of all that He is and has meant to millions down the centuries – He is gentle and humble in heart – and now this invitation, "come" is addressed to me. What does it mean to 'take His yoke'? – it means to be under His direction and care. He promises me rest – for my soul. I feel this rest – deep down rest – in the depths of my being – utter relaxation and restoration – rest from anxiety, care, and fear. I feel Him lifting my load from me – I can run up this hill now – I am at peace; I am happy, and life is much easier with His yoke upon me.

Other texts (that I have personalised) I suggest for use in this kind of meditation are:

'I will wait in hope on the Lord, and He will renew my strength. I will soar on wings like an

69

eagle; I shall run and not grow weary; I will walk and not be faint.' (based on Isaiah 40:31)

'I will cast all my anxiety on Him because He cares for me.' (based on 1 Peter 5:7)

'The eternal God is my refuge, and underneath are the everlasting arms.' (based on Deuteronomy 33:27)

'He is able to do immeasurably more than all we ask or imagine, according to His power that is at work within me.' (based on Ephesians 3:20)

'His peace He leaves with me, His peace He gives me. My heart will not be troubled, neither will I be afraid.' (based on John 14:27)

'I will not fear, for He is with me; I will not be dismayed, for He is my God. He will strengthen

me and help me; He will uphold me with His righteous right hand.' (based on Isaiah 41:10)

'When I call upon God, He will answer me; He will be with me in trouble, and He will deliver me and honour me.' (based on Psalm 91:15)

'God has redeemed me and has called me by my name. When I pass through the rivers, they will not sweep over me.' (based on Isaiah 43:1-2)

'God did not give me a spirit of timidity, but a spirit of power, and love and self-discipline.' (based on 2 Timothy 1:7)

Here are some specific verses to meditate on for healing of sickness and pain.

'For I am the Lord who heals you.' (Exodus 15:26)

71

'Who forgives all your iniquities, who heals all your diseases.' (Psalm 103:3)

Also helpful is the incident where the woman who had been haemorrhaging (bleeding) for twelve years is instantly healed as she touches Jesus' garment (Mark 5:24-34). And there are many more you can find or be shown.

I have suggested to many people over the years that they meditate in this way and have taught them how to do it. Testimonies have come back to me by the score that even pathological cases of soul-sickness have been healed through such meditation on God's Word, and all of us will find deep rest and peace in the midst of hectic, sometimes stressful lives, if we meditate like this at the beginning of every day. It is an important aspect of the search for total healing.

Are you a Christian?

Not 'Do you go to church?' though that is important but does not necessarily make a person a Christian. Nor 'Have you been baptised as a baby?' which does not necessarily make you a Christian. Nor 'Do you live a good life?' That does not necessarily make you a Christian.

A Christian is a person who has asked Jesus to forgive them all their sins and asked Him to come into their heart and life and asked the Holy Spirit to give them a new birth. So that the Christian life really is not only one of learning, or worshipping, or living, but experiencing the reality of the presence of Jesus the Good Samaritan, so that we can truly say:

73

'He walks with me and talks with me along life's narrow way. You ask me how I know He lives – He lives within my heart.' ('I serve a Risen Saviour' by A H Ackley, 1933)

For the Christian life, the church should be – and a good church will be – a place where you can find rest and find refreshment and healing. But the whole of Christian life, of prayer, worship, Bible study, teaching, and fellowship, if truly and sincerely engaged in, including receiving the sacraments of bread and wine, and of course being baptised, the whole of Christian life is therapeutic.

There has only been one entirely whole person who has walked the face of this planet; and that is our Lord Jesus Christ. All the rest of us need to be made whole in one way or another. But those of us who have taken Jesus as our Saviour; surrendered our lives to Him;

given ourselves to Him completely, and engage in all that the Christian life offers, in prayer and meditation, Bible study, and living lives for others to help and bless them, have found that the Christian life is in itself therapeutic.

The Christian life, according to the Bible, and in much experience over two thousand years, is a process of healing; the process of being made whole; of being transformed from faith to faith; from glory to glory. As Charles Wesley put it:

'Changed from glory into glory
Till in heaven we take our place,
Till we cast our crowns before Thee
Lost in wonder, love and praise.' (Love Divine, All Loves Excelling, by Charles Wesley, 1747)

That is the New Jerusalem – the heavenly Jerusalem – to which we are going. And if we are bleeding and dying on the Jericho road, and

all of us will have suffered pain in our lives, emotionally and physically, then the Good Samaritan will come to us and, as it were, set us on His donkey; in other words, He will carry us, He will help us, He will lift us up and He will take us on our way. And as we journey with Jesus, we shall indeed be made whole.

So far, I have been teaching about the healing of emotional, mental suffering, and pain. And that is extremely widespread in our modern society. But of course, it is only one kind of pain; and the other kind of pain – physical pain – can be just as intense or even more terrible to try to live with than emotional pain.

Now it is my sincere belief that if we are being emotionally healed, and are emotionally healthy people, this will be reflected in our

physical health. And I know this to be the view generally of the medical profession.

If we are negative in our minds, engaging in self-pity or excessive anxiety, or envy or jealousy, and mentally diseased, then our bodies will begin to reflect our mental and emotional state.

Even if our physical pain has a physical cause, such as arthritis, rheumatism or, in most extreme cases, cancer, even so, the physical pain will be intensified by mental or emotional distress; and conversely the physical pain will be lessened by mental and emotional wholeness, especially if we have found how to relax and let God into our innermost being to make us whole and healthy.

I have myself experienced intense physical pain, especially in my breakdown that occurred in 1983. It was an emotional and

physical breakdown through overwork, and I was told by my doctor that my intense chest pains were being caused by coronary artery spasms that in turn were caused by my terrible condition of emotional burnout and stress.

It was as I learned to relax into God and let Him make me whole in the very depths of my being, that these pains lessened, and one day, through the prayers of many, completely disappeared.

And so, as I teach in my book 'Total Healing', we are not body, mind and spirit separated into three separate compartments. All these three elements of our being, that constitute us as a living organism, interact with each other; and physical pain is real.

It is a fact that there are nerves all over our body - thousands upon thousands of them. And if we are in emotional distress, or

emotionally unwell, there is no part of our body that cannot be affected and made to feel painful, such as headaches and migraines caused by stress. So, it is important that we are spiritually whole and emotionally whole, because then we shall not have these thousands upon thousands of nerves in our body in some part or at some point or other expressing pain that we feel physically.

Below are further verses from Scripture, including personalised texts, for use in healing meditation.

'He will never leave me nor forsake me.' (based on Joshua 1:5)

'He is with me to the end of the age.' (based on Matthew 28:20)

'He healed many who were sick with various diseases.' (Mark 1:34)

'I will just touch His clothes and be well.' (based on Mark 5:28)

'My prayer of faith shall save me in my sickness and all my sins will be forgiven.' (based on James 5:15)

'He will work all things together for good for me, because I love Him and am called for His purposes.' (based on Romans 8:28)

'In the Name of Jesus, I will rise up and walk.' (based on Acts 3:16)

'The same Spirit of Him who raised Christ from the dead dwells in me and He will give life to my

mortal body through His Spirit dwelling in me.'
(based on Romans 8:11)

'If I ask anything in His Name, He will do it, so
that the Father may be glorified in the Son.'
(based on John 14:13)

'By His stripes I am healed.' (based on 1 Peter
2:24)

'Because I remain in Him and His words remain
in me, whatever I wish will be done for me.'
(based on John 15:7)

'I will ask, believe, receive.' (based on Mark
11:24)

'He will wipe away all tears from my eyes, for
there is no mourning, crying, or pain in that Holy
City.' (based on Revelation 21:4)

Choose a promise that most specifically speaks to your need. Believe it, embrace it, and absorb it into your soul.

Conclusion

We can be sure from the Scriptures that it is God's perfect will that we should be whole in body, mind, and spirit. However, we live in a fallen world; we have fallen bodies and fallen minds. We are imperfect from our conception in many ways. This I described at the beginning of this book as a beginning of our journey from Jericho to Jerusalem.

It is my experience, and the experience of others, that this journey should be with Jesus from as early as we can possibly know Him or hear about Him. Then although there are robbers, stealing our emotional or physical

health, as do bacteria or viruses with our physical health, and also the aging process, and many other forms of illness that show us that we are not perfect people, what the Christian faith says - what Jesus taught us - is that we are on a journey from Jericho to Jerusalem, and that if we live close to God through Jesus, the whole of our journey is a healing process.

There will be robbers; we cannot escape them. But there is no need for us to lie bleeding and dying on the Jericho road, because those of us who are Christians do not journey, like the man in the parable, all alone.

We journey with Jesus; we journey with our Christian friends. We have been taught the life of prayer and the life of love. And those of us who are Christians, though we know that the last enemy, as Paul says in 1 Corinthians 15:28, to be destroyed is death, until one day

when the Lord returns and defeats death, we shall die, nevertheless we do not want to fall off the tree of life like bad apples, but like ripe ones.

And so, we travel with our Lord on the journey of the Christian life towards wholeness in this life and are looking forward to the day when Jesus will make all things new; will make a new heaven and a new earth. And there will be no more pain; neither sorrow nor crying; and there shall be no more death. So, may this book help you on your journey, travelling with Jesus and let us look forward to the perfection of our being in realms beyond this, in eternal glory.

Amen.

Appendix

It is helpful to learn to relax if you do not already know how. The stresses and tensions of modern life affect nearly all of us and many people are not aware how tense they have become.

If possible, first practise this relaxation routine lying on your back on the floor, on a carpet and preferably free from draughts. When you have learned this technique, you will be able to do it lying on a bed, or even sitting on a hard upright chair.

- Lie with your feet a few inches apart and your arms loosely by your sides.
- Close your eyes.
- Feel your body heavy on the floor.
- Breathe deeply but naturally.
- Fill your lungs with air before breathing out.
- Now go through each set of muscles in turn, starting with your toes, first tightening them gently, then relaxing them: feet, calves, thighs, buttocks, abdomen, back, shoulders, arms, hands, fingers, neck, tongue, and eyes (imagine you are looking at a black velvet curtain).
- Listen to your breathing.
- Go through the muscles again, checking that they are still relaxed.

- Now either contemplate in your mind's eye a beautiful flower or perhaps a peaceful lake scene, or meditate on words such as 'Be still and know that I am God,' or 'peace, harmony, tranquillity'.

- After about ten minutes, go through the muscles in turn, this time tightening them gently. When you have done this, stretch like a cat and slowly get up.

Lightning Source UK Ltd.
Milton Keynes UK
UKHW020703080421
381640UK00005B/72